Late Midnight Walks

Late Midnight Walks

Thank you for existing

Thank you for buying my book

because of you, I get to follow my dreams.

Thank you from the bottom of heart..

Sincerely,

mubin.

Late Midnight Walks

Mubin Ap

self published

published online on various platforms

Edition 1st

isbn digital: 978-93-5737-715-7

isbn paperback: 978-93-5777-208-2

Authors Note

Writing a book is one hell of a task, one gets to writing and then hates what they have written, consequently, we then would try to edit it *which will make it a hundred times worse*. Armed with the knowledge that even four years and nine months aren't long enough to write a perfect book - here I am, presenting to you my book filled with imperfections. I've made countless revisions to this book, it feels like I started on a different book with a different theme and then ended with this one. I've spent so much time on this book that it has become a part of me and the imperfections that are present here are **my** imperfections. These are poems that reflect the way I see the world. It's crooked, warped and unstable. The reflections are shown through a comical house of mirrors.

Each poem is accompanied by a description that tries to explain the contextual elements regarding the poem. I believe that a poem or any piece of literature for that matter shouldn't be "too digestible" it shouldn't spoon feed the readers, I think that sort of writing undermines the intellect of the reader but at the same time I don't want my poems to be ones that could only be enjoyed by fancy schmucks with a wine glass and an artsy mustache (no offense to fancy schmucks.) I want to write things that can be understood by anyone who can read but at the same time I don't want to write something that is way too descriptive even though my writing style is descriptive. I'm not skilled enough to find the middle ground (yet) and the compromise that I've come up with is to provide contextual nuggets of wisdom regarding the poem so it'd be a good little read and hopefully a puzzle but with enough hints so that it can help one see the meanings behind those lines without needing shit ton of knowledge about literature. So the descriptions aren't exactly descriptions that explain the poems but rathers the story behind the poem, how it came to be and similar things that I wish to tell you.

Each of the poems presented here stands to represent the feelings one might come across at night. Feeling scared at night because of the darkness, imagining Lovecraftian beasts lurking there to catch you or the serenity one might feel when there is a beautiful and well lit night outside and decides to venture out to enjoy it. Even feelings like anger or love or misery that we might feel because for some reason we all love reading old messages from our bestie or an ex. watching videos (a shit ton of YouTube shorts) before sleeping has a huge potential to make us feel unexpected things and lastly, just remembering past bullshits and the idiotic things we've done and been through is enough to put us in a 'mood'. These situations evoke certain emotions and I'm really interested in what they are like. This book is simply those feelings but instead of being undefined – I tried to verbalize them. Words give shape to our thoughts and these poems are thoughts I've sculpted, given form and weight. From intangible to tangible, so you could touch them, feel the rough edges and appreciate the craftsmanship. If you didn't enjoy the book, that's cool too! This is my first book so I'm pretty sure there are several things that I've fucked up gloriously. I'd love it if you tell me what I messed up though. You can find my social IDs and even the link to my discord server on the last few pages, I'm not popular enough that if you tried contacting me - you'll be lost among the countless millions, so feel free to come over and chat for a while. Then, without any further ado – let's take a look at what this humble book of mine has to offer, shall we?

Edgy bastard

I made a sculpture out of blood
It rose to the heavens and above
It rained and painted the town red
A grizzly sight for one to behold.

I burned the world to grill some toast
I cried a river to drown all of you
I screamed out loud to burst your head
I broke your neck like a piece of twig.

Description

The world is a harsh place. I'm sure you've been hurt countless times before. When you're hurt, sometimes you feel as if you want to hurt those around you. I'm not blaming you, I feel the exact same thing. Broken people do have sharp edges.

I wanted to portray that feeling through this poem. I hope you feel the same edginess I felt when I wrote this.

The nights aren't long

The pale moon in a blue night sky,
And the unfaithful stars that wink at me,
The dog that couldn't sleep, just like me -
And we both walked beneath the night sky.

The familiar road and the familiar sizghts
But so unique when seen at night
Which I loved to be honest, it is dope
For some reason it filled me with hope

It calmed me down, the sights are cool
Took a breather and then another
But when I saw the night turn into day
I realised that my visit was overstayed.

Description

Some nights are too good to waste by just sleeping around and some nights don't let you sleep no matter how much you wish you could. I wrote this on a night where I couldn't sleep. I decided to dress myself up and go for a walk. It was past midnight and there wasn't much to see. As I was walking, the neighbourhood stray dog joined me in my nightly escapade. I was scared if it'd bite me but thankfully it didn't. I spent the night outside that day. It was fun. The next day tho..... It was horrible because of the lack of sleep.

My Love

The skies are so beautiful.

The clouds,

Never the same yet mesmerizing

How I wish to spent

Hours

Gazing at the beautiful sky

But I know, in my heart -

I have

You, my love. My personal

Ever-changing, mesmerizing and

Beautiful

World filled with wonders.

How I am lost spending

Hours

Gazing at your seductive eyes

Description

Love is a weird thing. It's confusing and convoluted. Who can we love? Who will ever love us back? What is it that we are actually feeling? Is it love or is it simply our hormones going haywire?

These are valid questions and despite how much science can point out what exactly love is - it remains a human experience. That is a statement said by a guy who advocates for scientific knowledge and practical thinking. Love is a human experience and humans by nature are one of the most mind bogglingly confusing and convoluted beings. So, who am I to blame love when I'm just as confusing as it is. I hope you will have a good time living your life, my friend. I hope you will enjoy your time living with the whims of an eccentric cupid. Never forget tho, just like how there won't ever be two same skies ever again, so do your love experiences.

Shine

Burn us like witches
Burn us on stakes
Misuse your power
TRY to burn us down

Cut off our head
Chop us into pieces
But keep this in mind
You can't ever rest

Burn us like witches
And watch us shine.
The minds of every generation
Will burn to their core

Cut off our head
Hope that we'd die
For every head that rolls
Watch a thousand rise

Burn us on stakes
And watch the flames.
We turn into beacons

And shine the way.

Chop us into pieces
And sew our mouths
But beneath our graves
You'll hear us sing aloud

We keep on fighting
For what is right
You won't shut us down
You won't lock us for long

You won't lock us for long

Description

People should have the right to wear whatever they want as long as it's not inappropriate within context. That's what I believe in. I don't find it okay to dress like a clown at a funeral and I certainly don't find it amusing to see someone getting forced to wear a hijab. I sure as hell am bloody pissed that there are these cunts who kill people over a fucking piece of cloth. These stupid ass morons. If they are what came of the winning sperms that made it then I loathe to even imagine how horrendous the failures would have been. These people need a grown up pacifier made of reused buttplugs.

Yes, I'm pissed.

I don't usually care much about anything but this is beyond unacceptable. It's inhumane and heartbreaking. Nobody deserves to be treated like this. Do what you wanna do and dress the way you want to but just try to be respectful towards others. Just have good common sense. There is a line to be drawn regarding what's acceptable and what is not. I think we can all agree on such a basic truth and keeping that in mind Iran just burned and abused this line, restricting its citizens rights to such a messed up degree.

Can't sleep

On the bed, I lay there awake
In a dark room lit by the moon.
Cuddling a pillow and hugging
The blanket. I laid there awake.
Sleep escaped my beloved mind
It eluded me like a fleeing thief.

I lay there awake dreaming
But not feeling sleepy, I dreamt of sleep.
Maybe I should count sheeps
One sheep, two sheep, three sheep
I led three sheep to be slaughtered.
Yet the land of dreams won't accept
The sacrifice, they won't let me sleep.

Description

As one might expect, this poem was written on a night where I hated not being able to sleep. Yeah that sucked! It is a harrowing experience to not fall asleep when one wants to. I stayed awake for most of the night and fell asleep at some point as if I had just simply blacked out. But before I passed out, I had the opportunity to write this poem. I tried to emulate that feeling of morbidity and the subtle despair I felt.

Ghost

Boo
I'm not scared you
Boooooo!!!
You're cute when you're angry too
B - boo ~
I'm not lying to you
Boo?
Yes, really.

The end
Boooooo

Description

I was scrolling through YouTube shorts and that is when I came across a video talking about a real case of paranormal activity. I don't believe in ghosts but when it's night-time and I'm alone in a pitch black and quiet room, I'm allowed to be a little bit scared. Like the idiot that I am, I imagined there is a ghost with me and that made things really really and needlessly hard. So yeah, to not piss myself.... I imagined that I'm flirting with a tsundere anime ghost. I'm not explaining that any further.

Night-time beast

In the night when silence Reigns
There comes the beast with a bloody teeth
The beast walks on two and has two arms
It's hoove - made of fire, the tail - of bones.
The beast makes no sound despite its size
It's a predator that stalks it's nightime prey
The beasts fur is a cloak of darkness
It's teeth, sharp, digs into blocks of steel
It's eyes are yellow and iris red, it's gaze
Can kill you like you're a measly fly
You better lock your doors and windows
And close your curtains. Pretend that
You are not there or risk everything
The beast will kill you and eat your soul
It will snack on your bones as it looks -

For its next nighttime prey to hunt

Description

I sometimes hate my mind and its ability to think of things that nobody asked for. Like the monster that I conjured up because I happened to hear something moving outside.

Missing something

Open me up
Take a look inside
Something is
wrong

Inside
I can feel it
Something
is missing

Cut me open
Take a look
Let me
bleed

Till I'm dead
It is fine isn't it?
For it all to
end?

Description

This is my attempt at a visual poem. I tried making it so that it makes somewhat of a sense when read both horizontally and vertically. I tried to give it a sense of lost identity which is represented by the detached and foggy lines. I felt like I'm not going anywhere in life. I haven't seen myself anywhere in 5 years. I don't even see myself in 5 years. Such a sense of identity crisis and knowing that I lack the talent or expertise gave life to this poem.

War

War, the fight no one wants
But the tussle every one is burdened with.

Not because they want to
But because they are forced to.

The intricacies of geopolitical rivalry
Or the intricacies of the greed felt by filth.

War, the fight fought by the ones
Controlled by the one drunk on power.

Description

Heard of the Ukraine vs Russian war. That left a bad taste for a while.

Lit cigarettes

I pulled and lit a cigarette
Nicotine seeping through my lips
In the cloud of smoke and ashes
I see the shapes of my troubles
As the clouds float away
All that remains is the pain
To cloud these thoughts
I pulled and lit a cigarette

Description

I've been trying to quit smoking. I'm seeing some progress in that regard and I'm extremely happy about it. I know this is a fight that many of us go through and I wanted to write about how hard it is to quit. The cravings are just one block in the countless things that make up the reason for why a person smokes. It's a choice, that's true, but sometimes it is the lesser evil. If you don't smoke then I'm sure you find that statement stupid. I don't blame that line of thought. I think you're blessed and I hope you remain that way. Nicotine is a curse that you don't want to dabble in.

A lone boy

A muffin with a candle on top
A kid singing a birthday song.
A muffin for one, nobody to share
A dim lit room, nobody's there

The rains drops clap
As the boy sings his song
The lightning smiles
When the boy blows the candle

The boy takes a bite
And tastes the muffin
The tears hid behind
His playful smile

Description

Despite how the content looks, I didn't write this one on my birthday or anyones birthday for that matter. I tried to imagine how many people will remember me 30 years after my death, that really put things into perspective. It's a poem about loneliness but the type of loneliness that one never gets to feel when they're alive.

Misunderstood

I imagine ghosts to be misunderstood
Lonely little ectoplasmic entities
Seeking nothing but a friendly hug
But with a curse, a touch of death.

Which reminds me of something
The extrovert buddy of mine
Friendly little annoying bugger
With a curse, a touch of death.

Description

You know by now that I'm a wimp. So it must not be surprising to hear that I succeeded in scaring myself once again. This time I tried not to succumb to the fear so easily and hence tried imagining them as.... Friendly. Like Casper the ghost. It even reminded me of this specific friend of mine.

But see, I have a chronic case of "fucking myself over" and so I once again imagined them to be deadly. That was fun ಥ‿ಥ

Procrastination

I kept running

Running from tasks

That I had to do

I wrote in runny lines

Hoped it would be funny alas

It wasn't

Fuck!

But procrastinating helps,

Helps in ruining

My life

But for real tho

I have to finish

This line and -

Description

I should probably clean my room. I should also try to write a bigger description for this poem.

To See Blood

I prick myself to see the blood flow
I like how red the blood looks
Reminds me that I'm alive
And that everything heals with time.

Description

Have you had moments where you've wondered whether you're truly alive? I've done so, this poem is the love child of my intrusive thoughts and existential crisis. Yeah! That's fun ain't it?

Bloody Fucking hell. The thing I hate about thinking too hard is that somehow I end up tearing open old mental scabs in an effort to heal myself. Oh the irony, I can almost taste the blood in my mouth. (get it? Cause blood tastes like rust…eh?)

Sweet Poison

A bottle of rum
Chug it down
Burn the guts
Puke it out
Laugh aloud
And fall down
A bliss to forget
A sweet blackout

Description

I don't have a problem with drinking. Never really felt curious about it enough to ruin my life or something. (I'm 21 when I'm writing this, give me time bruh, I haven't gone through enough shit to drown myself in alcohol) but I have friends who drink heavily. This is a poem dedicated to my buddy who texted me and then called me soon after because I was sleeping and didn't see his texts. He was piss drunk and emotional.

The only saving grace in this situation is that at least he had a good time.

The Past

The past
Tells us of tales
As old as
The world.
The past
Shouts our name
Out aloud
It talks about
Kings
And kingdoms
That fell
Or the ones
That rose to the
pinnacle.
It warns us about
The mistakes
We learned.
It tells us to be
Aware of our deeds.
The glorious days
And the times of
Endless pain.
Past holds both,

It wishes to be known.
The seekers seek.
The historians record.
The public reads.
The ignorant ignore.
The past longs to be known

Description

The things that already happened, they are not changeable, right?

I thought so but then I started to ponder over something else, if you can't prove something existed then did it really exist?

If you can prove that someone in the past really lived then did they really live? Did they exist?

The past is like a puzzle that has more than half of its pieces lost or hidden somewhere and we humans try to figure out the bigger picture somehow. Sometimes we find one of the hidden pieces and other times we speculate. It's really beautiful isn't it?

To Be Missed

How I loathe to be missed
But when the sun sets,
Knowing I'll be forgotten,
How I wish to be remembered.
To make a foolish bet,
Thinking I'll get the chips
I sat there holding the cards.
But soon everyone left.
soon I'm the only one left.
But soon
I'm
the only
one

left.

Miserably
fading into the mist

Description

Will someone retired, old and in the end phases of their life look back at their life and think "oh I wish I could see them again, they were great" and this mysterious person they're thinking of is you…. Just to be clear. Do you think it'd ever happen?

Will anyone remember us after our death? What about 60 years after our death? Then will we be remembered? Will anyone miss us? I don't necessarily enjoy being missed. I'm a living breathing human and anyone can simply text me and we could catch up. So hearing things like "aww I'm so glad you are back!! I MISSED you!!!" Piss me off. They didn't miss shit, what they meant to say was - i forgot you existed until just a moment ago but i don't want to look like an asshole so I'm gonna just say a crappy lie.

That being said, what if people just started saying things outright like "ah fuck here's he again, go away dude! We didn't miss you or anything!" That'd suck too tbh….

Even worse is knowing nobody will think about you when you're not there. When you're dead.

Hi(story)

Hi, hello uhm so how do I start?
Okay, wait.. I got it, let me try.
Black death, *achoo* or Spanish flu
Pneumonic, bubonic or septicemic!
Pick the plague that fits your grace.
Got a headache? Never fret my dear
I've got an all natural spear
That goes up your rear
Or a needle that'll touch your brain
But perhaps it's just the cocaine
Got a cough? A dry throat perhaps?
Poor sick kid swallowing heroine
Vlad the impaler and the murder queen
Vlad treats patients with impaling.
Are you depressed?
NO. DEPRESSION ISN'T REAL
You just need to eat some gruel
Wear a fake smile and cheer.
Ah what a time to be
The pleasant times of debauchery
And death and suffering and more death
That's the tale of history.

Description

Do you consider rap music to be poems?
R.A.P
Rhythm And Poetry

That's what I've heard it to be. It's sweet right? But the majority of people I've talked to in real life don't share that sentiment. So that gave birth to this monstrosity.

I'm not gonna degrade neither rap nor poetry by calling this either but…I love this thing. It has a weird choppy flow.

Gunpowder

There is darkness in our hearts
Dark and black, broken into dust
The powder lingers deep beneath
Waiting for a spark, to burst

Like a flag grenade, blowing up
Yet ripping people into shreds.
I just want to spread my wings
And go far, one way or another.

Description

People say that we need a spark in our eyes and a flame in our hearts. I'm just wondering if all sparks and flames are built equal. What if some sparks ignite something harmful? What if we have only one thing we can offer and that is to explode?

Exploding isn't bad either. Sometimes we should do what we have to do for the better good. What if the only way to be known is by sacrificing ourselves? What if we were wrong? And all we ever did was ruin lives. This is the dilemma of creating content. One could write something that despite its initial troubles could one day help someone or what if we wrote something that was initially well received but later in time ruined someone's life? It's hard but this is part of the job description I guess.

Late Midnight Walks

You can find my socials down below

|

Instagram: to_mubi

Twitter: to_mubi

That's it. Got no more socials bruh.

Dear Reader,

Thank you so much for taking the time to read my poetry book. It means the world to me that you would spend your valuable time immersing yourself in my words and thoughts.

I put a lot of effort into crafting each poem and it's truly a privilege to have someone take the time to read and engage with them. Your support and interest in my work means everything to me as a writer.

I hope that my words were able to touch your heart in some way, and that you found something meaningful within their pages.

Thank you again for choosing to read my book and for supporting me as a writer.

Sincerely,

Mubin Ap

Now that is said, I hope that I somehow managed to inspire you to write something. It's the dream of every writer to inspire someone isn't it?

I'm leaving a couple of pages for you to write something, this should be for you and it should a no judgment zone where you can write whatever you want without feeling any pressure.

So stay safe and keep writing!

Late Midnight Walks

Late Midnight Walks

Late Midnight Walks

Late Midnight Walks

Late Midnight Walks

Late Midnight Walks

Late Midnight Walks

Late Midnight Walks

Late Midnight Walks

Late Midnight Walks

www.ingramcontent.com/pod-product-compliance
Lightning Source LLC
Chambersburg PA
CBHW050025170726
48282CB00025B/544
* 9 7 8 9 3 5 7 7 7 2 0 8 2 *